Lost Sock

Written and illustrated by Tim Hopgood

Collins

These are my favourite socks.

I like them because they're spotty and because they're blue.

Blue is my favourite colour.

2

My socks are lucky.

Whenever I wear them we have fish and chips for tea.

Fish and chips is my favourite thing for tea.

But today isn't my lucky day. I can't find one of my lucky socks.
"Look in the wash basket," says Mum. But it's not there.

"It's probably under your bed," says Dad.
But it's not there.

"I know where your sock is," says Grandad smiling.
"It's in Sock Land! That's where all the lost socks go."

Grandad says in Sock Land, white socks float across the blue sky like clouds.
Socks of all colours hang from the trees.

And socks with holes in are carefully mended by the pretty sock birds that live in the sock trees.

But smelly socks are put in the cave where the sock dragon lives.
The sock dragon gets very angry if there aren't enough socks for him to eat.
Grandad says that's why so many socks go missing.

13

I'm worried that the sock dragon has eaten my lucky blue sock.

"Was it smelly?" asks Grandad.

"I don't think so," I reply.

"Well then, what are you worried about?
Your sock will be having a great time," he says.

But I wish my sock would come back.
We haven't had fish and chips for ages.

And then Grandad gives me a present.

It's a lovely new pair of blue socks.

And guess what?

I think they might be lucky ...

... because today we're having fish and chips for tea!

WANTED!

Smelly socks

To feed the hungry sock dragon

23

Ideas for reading

Written by Clare Dowdall, PhD
Lecturer and Primary Literacy Consultant

Reading objectives:
- be encouraged to link what they read or hear read to their own experiences
- read common exception words, noting unusual correspondences between spelling and sound and where these occur in the word
- predict what might happen on the basis of what has been read so far
- make inferences on the basis of what is being said and done

Spoken language objectives:
- select and use appropriate registers for effective communication
- use spoken language to develop understanding through speculating, hypothesising, imagining and exploring ideas
- give well-structured descriptions, explanations and narratives for different purposes, including for expressing feelings

Curriculum links: Art and Design

Resources: collage materials

Interest words: favourite, colour, dragon, enough, worried

Word count: 270

Build a context for reading

- Explain that this book is about a little boy who loses a favourite lucky sock. Recount a time when you lost something special and how it made you feel.

- Ask children if they have ever lost anything special and to explain to the group how they felt and whether the item was found again.
- Look at the cover together and read the title and blurb. Check that children understand what *lucky* means.
- Look at the interest words *favourite, colour, worried*. Model how to read longer, less familiar words using a range of strategies, e.g. phonics, familiar parts of words (*fav-our-ite*) and contextual information (colour, worried).

Understand and apply reading strategies

- Read pp2–7 aloud together as a group. Model how to read with expression and ask children to join in to bring the narrator to life.
- Draw children's attention to the speech marks. Ask them to find the speech on pp6–7 and to practise reading with expression.
- Discuss what has happened so far and ask children to predict how the story will develop. Will the boy find his lucky sock?
- Ask children to read to the end of the story, paying attention to the speech punctuation and using expressive voices. Support children as they read, intervening where necessary.

Develop reading and language comprehension

- Using the posters on pp22–23, help children to recount the events of the story. Discuss who has written each poster, and why they want to find lost socks.